HUNTER AND NOAH VS. SASQUATCH

SASQUATCH CHRONICLES
BOOK 1

PATRICK TALMADGE

HANGAR 1 PUBLISHING

HUNTER AND NOAH VS. SASQUATCH

"Hey Grandpa, I think I see a fire on the side of the cliff over there," said Noah. They had been going down the dry riverbed in Grandpa's mechanical riverwalker for three hours, and that was the first time they had seen anything out of the ordinary.

"Noah, I'm going to back up, so let me know when you see that fire," said Grandpa.

"Alright," said Noah.

When Noah saw the fire again, he let Grandpa know, and Grandpa shut down the riverwalker.

Grandpa looked at Noah's fire on the cliff wall and said, "Nice find, Noah, but I think it's the sun, not fire. I am not sure how the sun is shining through a solid rock cliff face, but it is time we checked it out boys", he added. "Before we head outside, I want both of you to make sure your suits are 100% prepared for emergencies, and I don't want to hear any grumbling. I know you checked them right after you put them on three hours ago, but repetition makes for perfection. So, no talking, do your safety checks, and then we can head outside."

"Hey Grandpa, you better not forget to do your safety check," said Noah with a laugh.

"I hear you, Noah. Don't worry, I'm doing my safety check as well," said Grandpa.

"Hey Noah, I think we better grab water and a couple of protein bars just in case we're out walking for a long time, and I'm hungry," said Hunter.

"Great idea, Hunter," said Grandpa, "I think we all better grab a snack before we head out."

"I hope we can try the jumping rope thing," said Noah.

"I think you mean the inertial reel safety harness, Noah," said Hunter.

"Yeah, that thing," Noah agreed, "I hope we can jump from trees and test it out."

Grandpa had taken a pair of youth Carhartt coveralls and transformed them into superpowered, spy-like, gadget-filled kids' dream clothing. The coveralls were waterproof and insulated and the kids could stay in freezing water for hours in comfort. Each suit had a fifty-foot inertial safety line, so they could jump from a tree or roof top and slowly lower. There were pockets with enough food for three days, purifying drinking straws, a built-in hydration bladder, an emergency medical kit, fire starters, knives, cable saws, and even a collapsible fishing outfit. These modified coveralls were a hiker or woodsman's dream come true. Grandpa was afraid of bears, so all the suits were designed to be used in trees. There were retractable safety cords built into the suits so that they could be attached to tree branches and used as a sleeping hammock. Even the boots had built-in retractable climbing spurs. Grandpa said if the suits were used properly and everyone did some hunter-gathering, there was no reason that a person couldn't last a few weeks in the suits, especially young boys who don't necessarily want to bathe.

While he was going through his safety inspection, Hunter thought about how he and Noah ended up here.

Two days earlier, their dad's company was looking for answers as to why a certain small valley in the cascade mountains blocks the most sophisticated radar known to man. Regardless of how many close flyovers by aircraft or even satellites, this one valley would block visual and electronic surveillance. They sent in three different research parties, and not one person from any of them returned. Once they were within one mile of the valley, electronic signals were beginning to be lost, and not one person from the party returned. Their dad thought of Grandpa's crawler and how it should be able to find out what was happening there.

The plan was for Grandpa to skirt the valley by following a dry riverbed that appears to run parallel to the valley, as shown in old forest service maps. None of the new maps that employed modern electronics for mapping showed the hidden valley. It showed up as a blurred mountain range. The original maps from the 1800s that used manual surveying showed the valley, but there was no mention of anyone investigating the valley. If Grandpa stayed far enough away, they thought he would be safe but close enough to make a visual survey. The plan was to stay outside the valley and look for ways to investigate the valley with a telescope. Dad wasn't worried because Grandpa's crawler was made from bullet proof Kevlar, had a home-built nuclear reactor Grandpa built out of old Xray machines, and could run a month without stopping if there was enough food and water. Their dad did not imagine his boys would sneak aboard with Grandpa on such a dangerous trip, or there never would have been a trip.

The boys knew that their crazy Grandpa was going on a trip into the woods in the crawler and they couldn't pass up a chance to wear their super-suits, so they did what any kid their age and with their unlimited imagination would do: they snuck into the crawler all suited up. By the time Grandpa found them, it was too late to turn around, and he had already lost radio contact with the kids' dad as soon as he got near the hidden valley. Grandpa knew he should go back, and his son would be mad, but Grandpa was known to be a bit eccentric but safety conscious, so he decided a great adventure was what the kids needed. It was not his fault the kids snuck aboard; he was just going to make the best of the situation. To be honest, Grandpa did not know about any of the potential dangers because they did not tell him about the earlier search missions or the lost persons. Had he known, he would have turned around as soon as the boys showed themselves.

The crawler is a mechanical-electric four-legged machine that looks like a four-legged spider. The crawler holds three people in a round pod that hangs between the legs. The operator hangs from the ceiling of the pod in a harness. There are actuators that connect their arms and legs to the crawler's legs. Basically, the operator hangs in midair and moves their arms and legs like they were walking on all fours to run the four legs of the crawler. It is all mechanical, with no electronics to get messed up if there is some sort of electronic blockage in the valley. The hydraulic actuators are mechanically activated as the operator moves. Grandpa designed this to work in outer space and did not want electronics near high electromagnetic fields, which could interfere with operations, so Grandpa made sure all components were mechanical.

1

THE OPENING

Hunter was brought back to reality once they stepped out of the crawler at the base of the cliff. As he got closer to the cliff, Grandpa could see the light better. It wasn't just a hole in the rocks, it was a large opening in the rock face. The sun must have been at the perfect angle for Noah to see the sun through the opening. *Looks like luck was with them*, thought Grandpa.

"Well, Noah, looks like you found the needle in the haystack," said Grandpa.

"What haystack?" asked Noah.

Hunter looked at his brother, buried his face in his hands and walked away.

"What?" asked Noah.

"Nevermind, Noah," said Grandpa, "we have exploring to do," and he walked up the steep bank towards the opening.

"What did I miss?" asked Noah as he followed Grandpa and Hunter up the hill.

The opening was twenty-five-feet above the dry riverbed. As he was walking towards the opening, Grandpa noticed the trail he was walking on was kept not natural. A normal trail is rough and has random rocks and holes. This trail was as smoothly racked as a fancy garden path. The trees along the trail were also trimmed to allow for easy access on the trail. Easy access for a huge basketball team. Grandpa wasn't tall, but the trees and bushes were trimmed to a height of ten feet. It would have taken a normal person a ladder to trim that high. Whoever did this wanted to make sure they had plenty of headroom or carried big things. The hairs were now standing up on Grandpa's neck. He was about to tell the boys to stop when they slipped between the rocks and disappeared into the opening. *Blast it! I was not paying attention*, thought Grandpa, as he hurried to catch the boys.

The inside of the wall was far grander than the well-maintained trail to the opening. Once he was through the opening, Grandpa stopped and stared. The boys had also stopped and were staring at the wonders of the valley.

There were decorative ponds, creeks, gardens, fruit trees, berry bushes, and shade trees, and it looked like what Grandpa thought the Garden of Eden should look. It was perfection, but who was the creator of this? As he stepped further out into the valley, Grandpa could see the valley went on in both directions for as long as he could see, and that was for miles in each direction. The valley was two miles across to the other side. It seemed impossible there was something in this valley blocking electronics. One look at his watch and Grandpa could see all his electronics were now gone. He asked the boys to check their watches and phones.

"Mine are not working," said Hunter.

"Mine are dead," said Noah.

"Well, that is not a good sign," said Grandpa. "I do not want to be in here without outside communication with you two here."

"Grandpa, we are not babies," said Noah.

"I know, Noah," Grandpa said gently, "but I want to make sure you make it into adulthood, so we are going to be cautious. At the first sign of trouble or something strange, we are leaving."

"Not going to be much weirder than a perfectly kept garden valley in the middle of a forest," said Noah with a grin.

"Well, there is that, Noah, but let's keep our ears and eyes open for weirder and maybe more dangerous things," said Grandpa.

"From this point on, I want both of you to always stay within ten feet of me. We have no radio to call for help, so we must rely on our own smarts and be observant one hundred percent of the time. Noah, this means no playing, all serious, all right."

"Understand, Captain," said Noah with a salute.

Hunter turned, shot Noah a single glance, and Noah immediately became serious.

"I understand, Grandpa," said Noah.

"Thank you, boys," said Grandpa, "now let's explore. We will walk up the valley to our left for twenty minutes. If we don't see anything unusual, we will head back the other way for another twenty minutes. I don't want to be here too long without communicating with the outside. Once we leave this valley, I think I need to head to an area where we can regain radio signals and contact your dad and let him know what we found and that you two are with me. I'm pretty sure I am going to get yelled at by your dad for not turning back right away, and if anything happens, I better not even show my face again," Grandpa looked slightly worried.

Hunter was most like Grandpa. Noah was relaxed and had no worries if he had a computer or was playing. Hunter loved athletics, video games, school and exploring. Hunter was also the planner, the one that seemed nervous, but he was quite observant. He said it wasn't that he didn't do anything wrong, it was more like he didn't get caught because he was so observant. He always watched Grandpa closely to see if there was anything going on he might miss. They had been walking for ten minutes when not Grandpa, but Noah reacted.

"What is it, Noah?" asked Hunter when he saw his brother stutter step and look off to his side. Grandpa stopped and turned to figure out what had grabbed Noah's attention in such a peaceful setting.

Noah didn't answer but continued to look at a clearing that held a single bench. This was not a normal-sized bench, but one twice the size a human would use. It looked like a tall table with a back.

"Finally," Noah said, "I swear I saw a huge furry thing sitting on that bench when we came around that bolder back there. One second, it was there, looking at me, and then suddenly it was gone. No sound, no smoke, just gone. I know if my Vuzix smart glasses were working, I could replay a video for you."

"Noah, did you skip your breakfast this morning?" Hunter asked. Hunter stopped mid-word as a figure began to appear on the bench Noah was talking about. As he watched, the figure began to look solid, and two more figures appeared, one on each side of the bench.

"Boys," said Grandpa, "please back up, and I mean now." Grandpa grabbed a boy in each hand and began backing up. The figures were now totally solid-looking, and they were huge. One look and Grandpa told the boys to sprint for the opening. The boys turned to run, but their way was blocked by more of the huge furry beings.

With a quickness Hunter couldn't imagine, Grandpa moved to stand in front of the new closer beings. In his hands, Grandpa was holding his special super bear spray. Grandpa was so afraid of bears that he developed his own bear spray. It could knock out a polar bear from one hundred feet away. He sprayed the four furry eight-foot-tall beings, standing forty-feet away, faster than the beings could react. Within two seconds, Grandpa incapacitated the four sasquatch-like things using his bear spray. Grandpa turned towards the three by the bench, and they were gone.

One more time, Grandpa yelled for the boys to run for the opening, and this time, the way was clear, and they all ran. Grandpa said as he was running, he didn't know what these beings were, but they were not bears. If he didn't know better, he added, he would say they were Sasquatch, but there isn't supposed to be any, at least until now, added Grandpa. Hunter had never seen his grandpa run but knew he had been a good runner when he was young. To be honest, Hunter knew he was having a hard time keeping up with Grandpa, so maybe Grandpa was more worried than he was letting on. Noah was a fast runner and was having no problems himself, but he wasn't worried either. Hunter was worried about how Noah would react in a situation like this since he was so young.

"They were about one hundred feet from the opening when suddenly there were dozens of sasquatch-like things surrounding them. It was as though they could appear and disappear at will," said Noah as he came to a stop with Hunter and Grandpa.

"Hey boys," started Grandpa, "I am a bit worried at this moment. I need you to keep your backs towards my back. We are going to stand back-to-back with you two holding onto each other and to me. We will spin around as needed as a group, and I will spray until I run out. I believe I have enough to take out this many of them, but if more show up, I am not sure what I can do," finished Grandpa.

The three of them stood together like that, waiting for the Sasquatch things to attack for over five minutes before Grandpa suggested they might be afraid of his spray and they should make their way in this formation to the opening.

No sooner did they start moving than the Sasquatch mirrored their movements. As the minutes went by, more of the Sasquatch creatures appeared. None seemed aggressive and all are staying a safe distance from the trio, but it is obvious they will not let them near the opening. Grandpa told the boys it was time to try forcing their way to the opening. That he would start spraying, and they will all run towards the opening, hopefully taking the Sasquatch by surprise.

Without warning, Grandpa started spraying the Sasquatch. They were all within the one-hundred-foot range, and he expected them to fall as fast as the first four. This time the spray never reached the Sasquatch. It was like each one had its own invisible force shield, and the spray bounced off. When he saw the spray wasn't working, Grandpa threw the cans down, took a small box out of his pocket, and started spinning a handle on its side. It turned out Grandpa had an ultrasonic horn that was supposed to hurt a bear's ears, and he thought it might work here. For the first few seconds, it appeared the Sasquatch were in a bit of distress, but then they seemed to ignore it.

Grandpa is not using lethal methods and Hunter notices the Sasquatch are trying everything possible to avoid hurting them also. The Sasquatch could have rushed in at any time but decided to stay back. Just as he was thinking that the Sasquatch might be friendly, they began moving towards them. Using their sheer size and numbers, the Sasquatch forced Grandpa back out through the cliff opening. The sasquatch broke off large tree branches and was using them as push brooms to push Grandpa back without hurting him. The opening they had come through was beginning to get smaller as Grandpa was being pushed back out through it. Grandpa yelled to the boys just as the opening closed that he thought the Sasquatch could not swim or climb trees and, "to always, I mean always, travel downstream." The opening disappeared and Grandpa with it.

The Sasquatch had moved so quickly that in less than fifteen seconds, they separated the kids from Grandpa, which made their escape route disappear. There was no way to have imagined a situation like this, so Hunter didn't blame Grandpa. He was still trying to figure out what the Sasquatch wanted with them and not Grandpa. Hunter had noticed that the Sasquatch was doing everything possible not to hurt them. Then, there was his little brother. Noah made his tree-climbing toe blade come out so he could try kicking the Sasquatch. The sight was actually quite funny. Here was an eight-foot-tall Sasquatch holding ten-year-old Noah back with one huge hand, and Noah kept trying to kick the Sasquatch the whole time. The poor Sasquatch was looking at its fellow Sasquatch, pleading for them to help, and they were almost laughing. Hunter noticed all this and was confused as to what was really happening.

"Noah," said Hunter, "it's time to stop trying to kick the poor thing."

Noah looked at Hunter, up at the eight-foot-tall fur-covered Sasquatch, and casually said okay, then stopped, to the relief of the Sasquatch he was trying to kick. Suddenly, Noah took one more kick at the Sasquatch, which made the huge creature jump back and make a squealing sound, to the delight of its fellow Sasquatch. Noah laughed aloud, walked up to the big fellow, and offered his tiny hand to say he was sorry. The Sasquatch all silently witnessed how easily Noah relaxed in their presence. The Sasquatch looked at Noah's hand and made its own hand open to signal that Noah needed to open his hand so the Sasquatch could see it was empty. Noah laughed, opened his hand, and touched the hand of the Sasquatch.

2

ALONE WITH SASQUATCH

The Sasquatch did not make any sounds following the one squeal. The group of Sasquatch surrounded the boys using hand signals to let them know they were to walk. As they walked, Hunter talked to Noah. They had no idea what was happening or where they were going, but Hunter knew they were getting farther from Grandpa with every step. The valley cliff was too steep where they were to climb over and there were no more openings that he had seen since the last one closed. How the Sasquatch made the opening disappear is still a mystery. How they were able to make Grandpa's bear spray and ultrasonic horn ineffective was also a huge mystery. What are these things, thought Hunter?

When the Sasquatch had reached the area with the large bench Noah had seen the first Sasquatch, the boys were motioned to a short human-sized table next to the bench. There were baskets on the table with fruits and berries Hunter recognized, but he was not about to eat with the huge furballs surrounding them. For all he knew, the food was poison. Noah, on the other hand, was all for eating, as usual. Hunter warned him to avoid the food until he could figure out what was going on and why the Sasquatch wanted them. As Hunter was thinking, another smaller Sasquatch showed up and surveyed the situation. From how the larger Sasquatch acted, this new Sasquatch was either a leader or their mother. They kept dropping their eyes when it looked at them, almost ashamed, he thought. When the new Sasquatch looked at Hunter and his brother, he knew it was acting more like a concerned mother than a beast.

The smaller Sasquatch was still over seven feet, estimated Hunter, but much less muscular. He guessed it was a female Sasquatch, especially after it gently touched his shoulder and made hand movements like eating. He instantly felt relaxed and told Noah it was fine to eat. Noah dug in and the new Sasquatch smiled while they ate. Hunter wasn't sure what was happening but knew they were safe for now, and both he and Noah were hungry. They also needed to eat and keep up their energy if they were going to escape. After the boys ate their fill, the bigger Sasquatch motioned for them to follow them. He was confused, but Hunter knew they needed to escape these huge furballs and get back with Grandpa fast, regardless of whether they were friendly or not. He remembered Grandpa said these Sasquatch might not be able to climb trees or swim, which gave Hunter an idea.

The boys walked for an hour before the Sasquatch stopped at a small stream coming off the cliff wall. Seeing the stream reminded Hunter of one of the things Grandpa said, "Always go downstream." Hunter knew he meant that they should follow rivers or streams downhill, and eventually, they would find humans. After a short rest, the Sasquatch motioned for the boys to head to the other side of the valley. That was the opposite side Grandpa was on and Hunter wasn't happy about that. Ten minutes later, the group had to walk back towards their original wall to go around a pond. The pond was close to a thick stand of trees that stretched to the cliff wall Grandpa was over, and Hunter got an idea.

"Noah," said Hunter, "do you remember that video game with the squirrels that get away from the dogs?"

"The ramp run squirrels", asked Noah?

"The one and the same," answered Hunter.

"Any chance you see a squirrel ramp around here?" asked Hunter.

Noah glanced nervously around, then a sly smile spread across his face, "Maybe the one by the flat rock? It looks like a slide, and we could run up it,"

"I was thinking the same thing, little brother," said Hunter. "It looks easy in the video game, and we have log rolling spikes on the bottom of our boots that would give us the grip to run up the tree," he added. "I think that on the count of three, we both make our boot spikes click out and run for the log."

"With luck, Grandpa was right and they can't climb trees," added Noah.

On the count of three, the boys were ten feet from their target tree, which was leaning against bigger trees. Hunter guessed the leaning tree touched the other trees thirty feet off the ground. That gave them extra on their fifty-foot safety line. As Hunter called out three, Noah clicked his heels together to release the spikes and took off running. Hunter was a fraction of a second behind Noah as they ran up the angled tree. The Sasquatch was completely taken by surprise. They froze as the boys ran up the tree. Grandpa was correct, they were too big to climb. By the time the Sasquatch moved, Noah and Hunter were seventy-five feet above the ground and still climbing.

Hunter and Noah had spent lots of time in trees. Since Grandpa was so afraid of bears, he made sure the boys could handle themselves on the ground and in trees. Bears could climb trees, but the boys could swing from tree to tree or safely hang out of reach. The brothers always used safety equipment when climbing. Well, that is, except this time, neither of them hooked a safety line before running up the tree. Hunter was sure Grandpa would have understood under the circumstances. Even Grandpa would say no harm, no foul when he messed up and nothing bad happened. So compared to being on the ground with dozens of eight-foot-tall Sasquatch, running up a fallen tree wasn't too bad a risk.

Hunter had Noah climb until they were out of sight of the Sasquatch. The branches thirty feet off the ground were thick, and it wasn't long before they could not see the ground. He guessed they were seventy-five feet above the ground. Not only couldn't they see the ground, but they could not hear a thing through the branches. Hunter signaled to Noah that they were not to talk but travel across the treetops on the branches to the side of the valley. Hunter hoped the trees were tall enough to allow them to climb over to the other side. He had seen the irrigation water culvert on the map and thought it might be just on the other side of the valley wall. If it was, that was their ticket home.

They climbed up and down between trees for an hour before Hunter saw the valley wall and realized they were going to be able to make it over. Hunter paused while he decided on the best route to the wall. Noah was not having any problems and seemed to be enjoying the situation. Hunter thought how nice it would be to be as oblivious to danger as Noah was. He knew his little brother enough to know he was thinking how fun it would be to lower down on their safety ropes rather than the possible danger they were in from below. With that thought, Hunter wondered if the Sasquatch had been able to follow them from below. They would not know until they went over the wall and that the future would take care of itself, as Grandpa always said about the future and worrying about it.

Noah knew Hunter's plan. Grandpa said to go downstream and this irrigation water was going downstream somewhere, hopefully to a farm and away from these Sasquatch. Once at the bottom, they could send a search party to find Grandpa, thought Hunter.

Both boys inflated their coveralls and ensured the water-proof seals at the wrists and neck were properly sealed. Once they were ready, they climbed down the tree to a branch five feet from the water and jumped in. Hunter knew their heads were below the rim of the culvert, so they couldn't be seen from below, but kept his voice low just in case the Sasquatch were close. The water was moving slowly, Hunter guessed, not any faster than walking, but they were floating effortlessly and, more importantly, quietly.

After thirty minutes, Noah said he had a problem.

"What kind of problem," asked Hunter?

"My suit must have a leak because my leg is wet and cold, and I am shaking."

"You must have cut your suit when you were trying to kick the Sasquatch," said Hunter. "How much longer do you think you can stay in the water?" He asked.

"I waited as long as possible before saying something," answered Noah. "I need to get out and dry now, please."

"Alright, Noah," said Hunter, "give me a minute to plan." The trees were always thick around them, and Hunter had thought about how they were going to rest at night, so he waited for the right tree before he had them get out. The tree branch reached the top of the culvert, so it would be a stable way to get out. It was also a large tree with areas for him and Noah to sleep and stay safe. The most important feature was the top had been hit by lightning and had an eight-foot-wide flat area they could spread out on and stay out of sight from the Sasquatch.

After Noah and he were out of the water and up in the warm sunlight, Hunter took Noah's coveralls and laid them in the sun to dry. Sure enough, he had cut the water seal on one ankle. They had tape for the coveralls but nothing that would seal the ankle seam. Hunter thought about using the pitch from a tree but knew he needed to wait until the coveralls dried well enough for the pitch to stick. It was going to be warm enough for the next few hours that Noah's coveralls would dry, and he would not get cold. While the coveralls dried, they both ate a survival bar.

Noah accidentally dropped a piece of his in the water below and a fish grabbed it immediately. "Wait," said Noah, "Do you mean there are fresh fish in that water, and we are eating freeze-dried bars?"

"It seems that way, little brother," said Hunter. "Any chance you would like to try catching one?" he added.

"I am quite willing to try catching one, especially if it means not having to eat the rest of this bar," said Noah.

"I suggest you try using your bar as bait, seeing the first fish seemed to like it," said Hunter.

Both boys laughed as they got their fishing gear out. Hunter was correct, the fish were hungry and went for the bar bait. In no time, they had two large fish and set about cleaning them.

Noah looked at Hunter and asked if they had to eat it raw because he didn't like sushi.

Hunter laughed and said he had all that figured out and to just hand him the empty bar wrapper.

Noah looked at Hunter with a puzzled look, then handed his wrapper over.

Hunter took both empty wrappers, grabbed two other bars, and removed the wrappers. He carried the four wrappers over to the edge of their flat area and broke small branches. Once he was done, Noah realized he had made a nest out of branches that was lined with the foil wrappers from their bars. Then, he made two small wood grills for the top and placed the fish on the grill. There was just enough sunshine to cook the fish in their homemade solar oven.

"Later, we need to look for a large potato chip bag to make a bigger solar oven," said Hunter.

Noah was staring with disbelief at what his big brother had just invented and imagining how much nicer the fish was going to taste compared to the freeze-dried bars.

Hunter set the solar oven in the sun in the center of the old tree trunk. The trunk was soft, and he was able to dig a small depression to set the oven into so it would not fall over. Noah watched the whole thing, and Hunter was sure he was drooling. *All Noah thought about was food and computers,* thought Hunter.

"How long do you think it will take to cook?" asked Noah.

"Not sure," said Hunter, "but you might want to get your fork and knife out of your suit. While you're there, check and see if your coveralls are dry."

By the time Noah got back, he had his coveralls on and exclaimed they were dry enough for him and started rubbing his knife and fork together while making a goofy face. Hunter was glad Noah wasn't as nervous as he was. Hunter knew they were safe and was sure they would find Grandpa, but he was still worried, knowing it all rode on his shoulders. Best thing he could do was keep his worries to himself and his eyes open.

"Well, Noah, I think the fish is done," said Hunter.

Each boy took one of the small wood grills with a fish on it and silently ate. Hunter was grateful the Sasquatch had fed them earlier, knowing they only had the two fish right then. *Catching more fish would be easy if they stayed along the irrigation culvert,* thought Hunter. He needed to think of the best course of action to find Grandpa and stay safe.

Noah finished his fish, stood looking down towards where

he thought Grandpa might be, and said, "Don't worry, Hunter, you will figure this out like you always do." Without another word, Noah went back to the edge of the tree and gathered some soft evergreen branches. He looked at Hunter and said he was going to pick a cool spot to sleep that had a great view of the ground.

Well, I guess my kid brother is growing up, he is thinking about how serious this is, thought Hunter. *He's right, I can do this*. The best bet is to sit tight for the next day or two. They had everything they needed: a view of both sides of the wall so they could look for Grandpa and the Sasquatch. The more he thought about it, the more he thought it was the best bet to stay and wait. If Grandpa goes to get help, they will fly over, and being on the top of a tree like they were was like hanging a sheet out. As Hunter was congratulating himself, Noah called out for him to come quick.

Noah was jumping up and down, looking at his watch, saying, "Look, look, it's working, it's working." Hunter looked and saw Noah's smartwatch was lit up. He looked at his own, and it was also.

"I walked to the edge here, and my watch lit up," said Noah.

Hunter looked and realized they were at the farthest point on the treetop, away from the Sasquatch side. Maybe we are far enough that our phones work too. It was either the distance or maybe the burnt wood helps stop the Sasquatch blocking, thought Hunter as he pulled out his phone.

Hunter's phone didn't show a signal, and neither did Noah's, but Hunter knew their watches would not work without their phones getting a signal. That meant the phones didn't have enough to call out but maybe if he tricked the phones, they could send a short text to Grandpa. Hunter and Noah talked about all the tricks they knew to boost the phone's power.

They decided to use one of the foil emergency blankets to make a parabolic antenna. Then, they would turn off their smartwatches and smart glasses so no extra bandwidth would be used. Hunter would type a very short text to Grandpa on his phone because they knew they would have a fraction of a second to send any info before the phones shut down. Hunter then texted, "We escaped, going down h20." Noah turned his phone into a hot spot, and Hunter quickly connected to Noah's hot spot and pressed send on his phone. The boys looked at one another and then at their phones. The phones showed no signals, still, so the boys turned their watches back on and waited.

"My watch fired back up, but there are no bars," said Noah. "Just enough signal to send tiny bits of info to my watch."

"Same here," said Hunter. "Looks like we wait and see if we get any signals at night."

"I am going to finish my sleeping nest, then climb down to the water to wash and see if there is any sign of Grandpa," said Noah.

"Alright, Noah, but keep your eyes and ears open for the Sasquatch, too," said Hunter. "Remember, Grandpa might still be upstream trying to find a way, so don't worry if he isn't here tonight. Remember to hook your safety line before you begin climbing because we have enough problems without me getting yelled at because you fell," he added.

Noah built his bed, tied his safety line around a branch, and then climbed down the tree. He wasn't making any noise climbing, so Hunter relaxed. He knew even if Noah was on the irrigation culvert, he would be out of reach of the Sasquatch. He knew Noah was just a kid, but he was usually good at following directions. If Noah heard a noise, he would freeze and hide.

Ten minutes later, Noah came back to the top and exclaimed, "It was as quiet as can be down there."

"Did you see any sign of the Sasquatch or Grandpa?" asked Hunter.

"No," said Noah. "I used the flip out hearing cups in my hood and listened while I was washing. I heard a couple birds and maybe one of Grandpa's bears, but pretty sure the Sasquatch thinks we are still floating down the water."

"I bet they must have gone way downstream to check for us and went right past our nest. From below, I could not see a thing on the top of our tree. All the burnt parts made the top an umbrella that stops light," Noah added with relief in his voice. "But, if I know Grandpa, he is still up by where we came in trying to find a way in, so you are right, Hunter, he may not get here until tomorrow."

"I think we should stay here for two more days," said Hunter. "If Grandpa is up trying, we should stay and wait. If he goes by looking, then we need to keep a lookout. We should make a platform below us that we can lay on and not be seen by the Sasquatch."

"It needs to look like a nest," said Noah. "That way, we will be under cover, would look like an eagle's nest, and be totally cool."

Hunter laughed at his brother, but it was a great idea. They would be hidden from below and on the sides but be able to see over the edge. Grandpa's walker isn't loud, but they should be able to hear the feet as it walks in the rocky dry creek bed, or dirt, from a few hundred feet away. That would give them enough time to climb down the tree to meet him. "Great idea, Noah," said Hunter, "and that should be our first task in the morning."

"After fishing and eating," Noah rubbed his belly, "because I work better on a full stomach."

"Dad's right, Noah, you are a bottomless stomach," said Hunter.

The boys laughed for a bit while they finished preparations for the night's sleep. Their coveralls were going to be more than warm enough for the mild night's temperature. The focus was extra evergreen branches for padding, then making sure there were strong branches to clip their safety straps to. Both boys had slept in the treetops before and sometimes, when the weather was bad, they made hammocks and slept lower. Tonight was clear, but they needed to stay out of site from below, so even if it were raining, the boys would have slept on the top. The coveralls can handle cold water, so a warm night would be no problem.

Light was almost gone as the boys clipped in for the night and said goodnight to one another. Hunter looked at the stars, remembering there would be no moon tonight, so it would be a dark night. His last thought as he went to sleep was how he had to remain calm. Grandpa always said, "don't waste time worrying about the future. The future will take care of itself".

3

THE FIRST MORNING ALONE

The sky was beginning to get light as Hunter opened his eyes for the first time. He had slept through the night, which meant there had been no weird night noises. He was always the first to awake from noises while camping. He knew it was because his hearing was so good, but Grandpa teased him about being afraid of bears because Grandpa really is afraid of bears. He smiled, thinking about their grandpa, but knew that he was going crazy worried about them at this moment. Hunter knew he had to think like Grandpa would so they had a better chance of meeting up.

The last of the stars disappeared into the morning light as Noah made his first morning grunts. He rolled over and looked at Hunter, "When's breakfast?" he asked groggily, then laid his head back down.

Hunter smiled, knowing Noah was doing fine, even though he was worried in his own way.

"If you want to eat, you might want to climb down and get some because I don't think they were intending to come up by themselves," Hunter teased Noah.

"I can't believe how lazy fish are," Noah groaned as he unclipped and stood up. "You know what, Hunter?"

"What?"

"I could live here forever! Mom's not here to make me take a shower, I can go outside and not get yelled at, and I can eat fish every morning instead of eggs," grinned Noah as he dropped through the branches with his fishing gear.

"Good luck, brother," Hunter called after him, "And hope you remembered the bait!"

"Dang," Noah's head reappeared from behind a branch, "Mind handing me the bar pieces, big brother?"

"Try catching at least four fish this time," instructed Hunter as he handed Noah the bar pieces. "We are going to be here all day, and fish tastes better than the bars."

"You are one hundred percent correct," said Noah, "and I will do my best to be a fish slayer." With that, he was gone again.

"Remember to clean the fish there and do not let any fall on the ground, or we could be caught," said Hunter as the head slipped below.

To Hunter's surprise, thirty minutes later, Noah returned with six good-sized fish. Noah was also surprised that while he was fishing, Hunter had built a bigger solar oven using his foil space blanket. The new oven was large enough to cook all six fish at once. Noah stood and stared at the new oven, "We eat like bears today."

Hunter laughed as he placed the fish on the new, larger grills. There was no flame, so the thin stick wood grill would not burn. The biggest problem would be the smells. Hunter was sure the Sasquatch had a good sense of smell, so it could attract them if they made a mess or their cooking was too smelly. He was sure the smell of raw fish would not be noticed, but cooked fish might raise flags. As the fish cooked, Hunter paid notice that in the early morning, the warm smells rose with the winds. He would have to watch during the day to see how the temperatures affected the wind so he could keep the smells down.

While the fish was cooking, Hunter was thinking about their next moves. He knew they were going to stay there all day today and maybe tomorrow. They were safe, Grandpa was most likely to head down stream like he taught, but they needed to look for more food. Fish tasted great, but they needed more to survive and be happy. He decided to tell Noah that they were going to go to the ground after breakfast and do some food gathering. The berries, mushrooms and even a few of the dandelion greens might help if they got desperate. Noah was more than happy to do forest food gathering.

"Duh, it's food," he said.

Hunter shook his head and dished up their morning fish. After they ate, Hunter made sure they both did a safety check on their suits. They decided the cut in Noah's boot seal was unsealable, so floating to safety was out. That meant everything else had to be in perfect order when they finally left. Once the safety checks were complete and the nest items were secured, the boys clipped in and climbed down the tree.

The first step was to the irrigation culvert to wash. Hunter reminded Noah to wash well because they had eaten fish, and bears love fish. If he smelled like fish, the bears would smell him and be attracted. That was enough to cause Noah to triple-wash in the water and roll in the evergreen needles at the base of the tree once they reached the ground. Hunter decided his brother was being smart. Human hunters and animal predators often do the same to cover their scent. Hunter joined Noah, and the two rolled around until they felt "smell-less," as Noah said.

Hunter had already told Noah they would not talk unless it was an emergency. That meant Sasquatch, bears, or Grandpa, so the boys quietly searched the ground around their tree for mushrooms. They decided to look for mushrooms first, then berries. The mushrooms would be near the trees and logs. The berries would be in the clearings. Grandpa and their parents loved mushrooms and hunted them, so the kids knew which ones were good, and as Noah said, "were his favorites and he could have all he wanted because mom wasn't here". The early morning was quiet, and the boys were able to collect a good quantity of mushrooms in thirty minutes. With the mushrooms picked and hauled up to the tree top so there was no hint the boys were there, they cautiously walked away from the safety of the tree to find berries.

The Carhartt coveralls had two pull-out forest gathering bags perfect for berries, which Grandpa built in. The boys were lucky that the berries were close, but the best berries were out in the clearings. Hunter decided Noah would stay closer to the tree line, and he would move out further into the clearing. Noah would pick, but he would look for danger more than pick. Hunter would pick as quickly as possible and be back to Noah sooner. They were only one hundred feet apart, but Hunter was on full alert as he picked. The berries were thick, and within ten minutes, Hunter had gathered enough berries for two days of heavy eating, even if Noah was hungry. Noah had also found a good number of berries, and the boys walked back to the tree feeling successful.

The walk to the tree was uneventful, and the boys clipped on their safety lines and headed up the tree. They washed the mushrooms and berries and then headed up to the nest. As they were climbing, Hunter told Noah he had seen a small river about two-hundred feet further away when he was hunting berries.

"Why don't we go down there later in the afternoon? We can see if there are any freshwater clams or crayfish." Hunter suggested.

"That would really make for a balanced diet and be yummy," said Noah as they reached the top.

After resting and eating, the boys headed back down the tree. They washed and then took plenty of time to survey the area below the tree on either side of the cliff. When Hunter was sure it was safe, they climbed down and headed towards the river. They kept to the trees and the taller bushes as they approached the river. The river was fifty feet from any bushes, so after pausing to ensure it was clear, they bent over and hid behind the bigger river rocks. The river had nice pools that looked promising for both clams and crayfish. Noah's boot leaked, so it was Hunter's job to go in and look for food, while Noah stayed low by a boulder being the look out.

Hunter held up the first few clams he found in the sand by

the shore, and Noah almost yelled but caught himself just in time. Hunter knew the clams would stay alive in their irrigation water, so he gathered enough for the next two days. Once he had enough clams, Hunter turned his attention to the crayfish gathering. Both he and Noah liked crayfish. *They tasted like lobster and who doesn't like lobster,* he thought. Hunter had to be in deeper water to gather the crayfish, which meant he had to put his arm all the way into the water up to his shoulder. Sometimes, his face got wet, but it was going great until he stepped into a hole trying to grab a crayfish.

Hunter stumbled and went face-first into the river. His coveralls were water proof, so the water wasn't a problem, but the crayfish he was reaching for was. Hunter had grabbed the crayfish as he fell and had not let go as he fell in. The issue was that the crayfish had also decided to hold on to Hunter. A crayfish is a small freshwater lobster-looking thing with pincher claws. They may not be as big as a lobster, but in cold water, and being a slightly scared thirteen-year-old alone in the woods with a ten-year-old brother, surrounded by Sasquatch, can make the crayfish claw pinch seem a million times worse. When Hunter stood back up with the crayfish holding onto his pinky finger, he let out a howl that would have made a wolf proud.

Noah started laughing right away at the sight. Both suddenly froze when they realized what they had done. Hunter climbed out of the river, they silently crept back to their tree and went straight up. They nervously lay listening for over an hour, occasionally looking over the edge of their nest. Hunter was the first to break the silence.

"Noah, I am so sorry for yelling," Hunter looked dismayed.

"I understand, Hunter," said Noah, "If that crayfish had grabbed me, I would still be running down stream screaming. It was funny, though. The look on your face was perfect, and I lost it myself," he added.

The boys relaxed and laughed while they kept looking for Sasquatch and Grandpa. Hunter got up and emptied his clams and crayfish onto the solar oven grill. While he was cooking, he told Noah to pull his pliers out of his tool kit because he would need them for the crayfish.

"I wonder if Grandpa was a Boy Scout," Noah mused.

"Why?" asked Hunter.

"Well, he thought of everything for our coveralls," said Noah. "I mean, who would have thought of putting a special tool in our Carhartt's just to eat crayfish? Our Grandpa is smart, he is prepared for everything, just like a Boy Scout," Noah's face was furrowed with total seriousness.

For the millionth time in his life, Hunter buried his face into the palms of his hands after something Noah said. He thought there wasn't anything to say after that, so he kept cooking, hoping his brother was ok.

The boys spent the rest of the day eating and on the lookout. Fortune was theirs, and no Sasquatch showed. Although Grandpa didn't either. Hunter now knew what bittersweet meant. After dinner, the boys went down and washed in silence. Hunter could hardly believe their luck that they lost the Sasquatch, but still, no Grandpa was a bit worrisome. They would stay tomorrow, and if Grandpa hadn't come, they would follow the irrigation culvert down. It seemed to be the safest route. Fish, water, and an escape avenue if Sasquatch shows up. Also, Grandpa said always go down stream, so they would stay the course and follow the culvert.

They spent the next day in their treetop, eating the rest of their foraged food and looking out for Grandpa. While they waited, they decided that after they headed out tomorrow, they would go to the stream and gather more crayfish and clams. Aside from having enough good food, Hunter and Noah thought the river might be far enough away from the Sasquatch valley that their phones might work. Their coveralls have solar panels built into the shoulders, so their phones, watches and smart glasses always stay charged.

Maybe Noah's right about crazy Grandpa being smart? Yes, smart and a bit crazy, but at least mostly harmless, Hunter thought with a grin.

4

DAY THREE ALONE

The night had been uneventful, not even animal noises woke them. When the boys awoke, they gathered their gear, ate breakfast, and headed down the tree to wash. After cleaning up everything, they scratched a note in the dirt next to the tree that stated who they were and where they were going. The note was for Grandpa or whoever might find their tree in hopes they would follow their path downstream. The last thing they did was stack rocks around the note to protect and draw attention to it. Noah insisted they make arrows so that Grandpa would know what tree, so they added arrows pointing towards their tree.

With the note completed, the boys headed to the river to do some foraging and try out the phones. The phone idea was a total bust. Not even the watches worked, so after filling their bags with mushrooms, crayfish, and clams, they walked back to the irrigation culvert and headed downstream, hoping to find

Grandpa or at least a way away from the Sasquatch. They at least needed to get to an area where their phones worked if they had any hope of rescue or contacting Grandpa.

Noah had wanted to head back up stream to where we went into the valley with Grandpa. Hunter argued it was a bad idea because they knew the Sasquatch had to have a lookout there, otherwise, they would not have seen us the first time. They followed Hunter's logic, heading downstream, hoping Grandpa would see the message by the tree.

The boys decided to walk the hillside alongside the irrigation culvert. Hunter felt it offered the best vantage point and escape route. The culvert was usually one-hundred-feet above the dry riverbed, which gave a clear view below when they looked but kept them hidden. In an emergency, they could jump into the culvert water if needed. The plan was solid. If they wanted, they could also climb a tree to look over the cliff wall into the Sasquatch valley. Hunter thought they would be able to sneak looks from trees rather than climbing the cliff wall, where they could fall or make too much noise.

Before leaving the tree that morning, the boys agreed to stay silent unless there was an emergency. From what Hunter could best guess was three hours because his phone and watch were still blocked, he signaled for them to stop. They had stopped under a huge maple tree that had branches that went over the wall into the Sasquatch valley. Hunter whispered that they were going to climb up the tree and check out the valley on the other side. If all was quiet, they would stop for a while and eat lunch. Noah suggested Hunter prepare the solar oven, and he would climb to check it out. Hunter agreed because he knew Noah was an expert climber and would use his safety rope. Sure enough, Hunter watched Noah secure the safety line before starting up the tree.

Good kid, thought Hunter, *I taught him well.* And began assembling the solar oven.

By the time Noah came back down, the oven was set up, and two fish, some clams and crayfish were already laid on top. Hunter also had berries and mushrooms washed and ready to eat. Noah thanked his brother and then dug in. By the time Noah and Hunter had eaten the berries and mushrooms, the rest of the lunch was cooked. Neither boy talked much. Both knew they had to be silent and were a bit scared. After eating, they washed up. Hunter knew Grandpa was more scared of bears than needed, but cleaning up after eating fish in the woods was very important. If there were any bears around and smelled fish, they would be attracted, which was not something Hunter wanted while alone in the woods with Noah.

After lunch, the boys walked for what Hunter assumed was four to five hours. The sun was beginning to get lower, and he knew there would be just enough light to cook dinner if they made camp now. They had come to a tree that would be perfect. Noah climbed the tree to get things ready for the night while Hunter caught fish. When Hunter reached the spot Noah had chosen, he found Noah had built nice nests for both and even cleared out the kitchen area. While walking, Hunter had seen that one side of the tree facing West had broken away, which he hoped would make an open space the sun could shine through and cook their dinner. Looked like their luck was holding.

After eating, the boys dropped down to the water to wash

up. They talked softly while they kept their eyes and ears on alert. Tomorrow, they would continue heading down stream after gathering a few mushrooms and berries for the morning. The area below the tree by the dry riverbed was quiet. Hunter was wondering if these woods were always this quiet or was something scaring them. He was sure he and Noah had been quiet, but maybe a predator like a bear was close. For now, they needed to climb back up the tree and get secured into their sleeping nests. Tomorrow meant more walking and hoping to find Grandpa or get cell reception.

5

DAY FOUR AND THE EXCITEMENT BUILDS

The first light of the morning was coming through the maple leaves, and Hunter glanced around their tree nest. Noah had done a great job of lacing smaller branches into mesh nests for each of them. All they needed was to add extra leaves to cover the bigger branches, and their suit was padded enough to be comfortable. As he was enjoying the cool wind on his face, Noah sat up and stared off into the distance. Hunter sat up, pulled his hood up over his head, pulled out the built-in ear cups, and listened. Noah pulled his hood up and listened.

The boys heard a faint noise which sounded like a rock being kicked. They had heard deer in the woods, but this was a much louder sound, and Hunter knew it also sounded too loud for a bear. Whatever it was was huge, which meant it was a Sasquatch. A normal black bear is six foot tall, one-hundred-seventy-five pounds, and these Sasquatch are eight-foot-tall and over eight-hundred pounds. No matter how they walk, the Sasquatch are so heavy they make noise. Hunter was sure it was at least one Sasquatch. They would have to wait and see if there was more than one and if they had been found.

Hunter had just said they needed to sit still and not make a sound when Noah stood up, clipped his safety line around a branch, said, "I am not running anymore", and jumped.

"Well, I didn't think that all the way through," Noah muttered, looking down while he was speeding towards twelve huge Sasquatch below. Luckily, he stopped himself twenty feet above their heads. They were walking looking forward and didn't see or hear him. They were so big that the sounds the twelve of them made walking blocked out the noise Noah made on his decent. Noah knew he dared not make a sound but didn't want to hang out in the open, so he pulled out the tool to crank himself back up. The mechanism was quiet, and he felt the Sasquatch were making too much noise to hear him anyway. He was about to push the tool into the slot when it slipped through his sweaty fingers towards the beasts below.

Noah almost cried out as the tool fell but closed his eyes, shut his mouth, froze, and prepared for the worst. He didn't dare breathe or move; he could only wait for the trouble to start when the tool hit the ground. He could hear the Sasquatch walking below. They never missed a step or slowed down by the time Noah couldn't hear them anymore. He took his first breath and slowly opened his eyes. The last Sasquatch of the group was disappearing further down the wall. For a reason unknown, they had not stopped when the tool fell. The problem now was Noah had to figure a way back up since his cranking tool fell.

He took a deep breath, thinking he had to drop to the ground to get his tool, when he saw where it had landed.

His cranking tool wasn't on the ground below. By some miracle, the tool had fallen, and the handle slipped into the tear of his boot seam. If he had not torn it when he was kicking the Sasquatch four days ago, it would have hit the ground, and he would have been caught. Still, Hunter was going to kill him when he cranked himself back up. *It wasn't his smartest move but might be the luckiest,* he thought as he cranked himself back up to accept his punishment.

The look on Hunter's face almost made Noah release and drop to the ground, where he thought it might be safer with an eight-foot-tall Sasquatch than a mad older brother. To his surprise, Hunter didn't yell, he grabbed Noah and hugged him.

Hunter looked down at his little brother and shook his head, "Noah, it is a good thing you are luckier than you are impulsive. If I tell anyone what you just did, you will be grounded until you are forty years old."

"Thank you for not yelling, Hunter," said Noah.

"Noah, there are things coming our way as we work our way out of this mess that are way worse than that silly jump of yours. As Grandpa would say, "No harm, no foul". Although I am sure this is one of those stories we will get to tell our kids and grandkids someday, but not necessarily our parents or Grandpa, at least right away," Hunter added with a knowing smile.

"I am sorry for doing that, Hunter. I was scared, frustrated, got mad and lost my temper," said Noah.

"I know, little brother. I am scared, too, but I know if we

follow everything we have been taught about surviving in the woods, we can make it out. Also, we have Grandpa's converted Carhartt coveralls to keep us safe."

After the close call, the boys sat in the tree and ate; after an hour, Hunter felt it was safe enough to go back down. Noah had dropped into the Sasquatch valley, but the boys stayed on the irrigation culvert side, especially since they knew there were Sasquatch nearby. Grandpa would need to stay on the dry riverbed side with his crawler. The boys kept to the plan and climbed down to the culvert.

They caught six fish, and Hunter set them on the solar oven next to the culvert. They decided to stay on the ground to cook while the Sasquatch were nearby. While the fish cooked, the boys walked down hill to the dry riverbed to gather berries and mushrooms. The river was too far away for Hunter to feel safe. They could catch more clams and crayfish later.

"Time to think safety now and food later," Hunter told Noah.

Noah, who had decided after his close face-to-face with eight-foot-tall furballs, was ready to think a bit before he acted.

"Nice decision," Noah agreed. "This is a bit more real than our VR video games, and if we are going to win, we need to think first act later. Like they say, 'measure twice, cut once,' so we will think twice and act once."

The boys were quiet the rest of the time they hunted. The fish was nicely cooked by the time the boys reached the culvert. Both were still shaken from the excitement and ate in silence. After eating, they packed the remaining food for later and washed up. Before they started walking again, the boys scratched a note into the ground below the tree and surrounded it with rocks, including the arrows Noah had insisted were needed. Hunter hoped their notes were easy to see because this tree was a bit further away from the dry riverbed Grandpa would come down searching.

6

GRANDPA DECIDES

Unknown to the boys, Grandpa had spent the first three days trying to get back into the valley. After failing to get through the wall, he tried going over, but an invisible force field stopped him. Finally, on the fourth day, he gave up trying. He decided to head downstream in the same direction they had been traveling. He knew if the boys escaped, they would try to head downstream - if they listened to his teachings, that is. Downstream was where he would reach civilization sooner. Grandpa climbed into the crawler and went to find the boys.

Grandpa had tried every way possible to get into the valley. It would take a bomb to break through that wall if it was possible to get through the force field. Grandpa knew science, but he had never heard of a working forcefield. Although four days ago, he had never seen a Sasquatch either. This was turning out to be stranger than he expected, and it most likely was going to get even weirder. With that thought, he headed down stream to find his grandsons.

He had been traveling half the day when he saw something that caught his eye by a tree. Someone had stacked rocks around a tree, including arrows pointing at the tree base starting from thirty feet away. Whatever it was, someone wanted it to be seen. Grandpa shut down the crawler, checked his suit and headed outside. After reading the note, Grandpa dropped to his knees. Now he knew the boys were safe and were heading downstream. It was close enough that Grandpa knew this was where they spent their first night. They had not written a date, so Grandpa was not sure when the boys wrote the note and left. It could have been anytime in the last three days. He would have to proceed slowly so he didn't miss them.

Grandpa was torn between heading out to get help and trying to find the boys. He decided that he needed to keep heading downstream because he knew the boys were headed that way, and there was no way he could leave. His only hope was to find the boys or get to an area where he could get phone reception and call for help. It really was a no-win situation because no one knew about Sasquatch or that they had advanced technology. His son would have to forgive him for whatever decisions he made. This was a situation that had never been experienced before. Grandpa thought about heading away from the Sasquatch valley to get clear of the signal blackout, but the area around was too mountainous. His crawler was outfitted to travel dry riverbeds, not climb mountains.

"Please think before you jump, boys," said Grandpa as he climbed back into the crawler and headed downstream.

7

HUNTER AND NOAH CONTINUE

Hunter and Noah were talking as they walked, unaware that their grandpa was now on his way to find them. They knew the Sasquatch were looking for them, but they couldn't be sure if the Sasquatch would try to come to the culvert side. They knew they could jump into the water at least for a while before Noah needed to get out. Being by the culvert seemed to be the safest, and it also supplied the fish and water they needed. They decided to walk on and hope they never saw the Sasquatch again.

After three hours of walking, Noah pointed to the river at the base of the hill. It was now within three hundred feet and a safe distance for them to travel away from the culvert.

"I was hoping to get more berries, clams, and crayfish for the trip," said Noah after pointing out the river.

"Great idea, Noah," said Hunter, "We need a break and the food."

The brothers gathered extra berries and mushrooms, then headed to the river. Once again, Hunter oversaw the clam and crayfish collecting because of Noah's leak. Noah would later admit he was hoping Hunter would get pinched again because the first time was so funny, but no such luck. Neither felt an urgency to start walking and spent an extra two hours relaxing by the river before heading back up the hill.

Before starting out, the boys ate cold fish, berries, and mushrooms. They would save the clams and crawfish for that night's dinner. Once everything was cleaned and packed up, they headed downstream. Four hours later, Hunter found a great tree that fit their needs, and they stopped for the night. The tree was a bit smaller than the first two, so they cooked next to the irrigation culvert. Hunter liked it better down by the water because it was easier to clean up before bed. As usual, Noah climbed the tree and prepared things for the night while Hunter prepared dinner.

Hunter was busy laying the food onto the new stick grills he had built, preparing to transfer it to the solar oven rack, when he heard a rustling in the bushes below the culvert. His first thought was that Grandpa had found them, and he stood up quickly to look. He almost fell into the culvert when he saw what made the noise. A mother bear and two cubs were climbing up the hill right towards them. Towards them, their fish, clams, and crayfish.

Hunter yelled to Noah that there was a bear and two cubs coming. He needed to be prepared to transfer trees depending on what the bears were going to do. Hunter knew better than to grab any of their food before climbing up to Noah. The bears wanted the food, not the boys. Hunter grabbed his solar oven and headed up to Noah. The bears can have the fish because they can catch more, but the solar oven was not easily replaced.

From thirty feet above, the brothers watched the bears devour their food. Noah wasn't as mad as Hunter thought he would be.

Noah was fascinated with the bears. He could see why Grandpa was afraid of them, but with their suits, they could easily stay safely away, so Noah was enjoying the experience.

"Too bad we didn't have any more fish to feed the babies," he said, as he started slipping forward over the edge towards the bears. He had his safety straps attached, and Hunter grabbed him, so he only fell a foot. It was a foot he would never forget, and now Noah had a clear understanding of Grandpa's fear of bears.

After making sure Noah was safe, Hunter rolled onto his back and fell into a fit of laughter. Noah was still breathing like he had finished a running race, and his pupils were the size of cups. Hunter knew he should worry about the bears, but he assumed they ran away as soon as they heard his uncontrolled laughter, and he couldn't stop anyway.

After a minute, Hunter's laughter subsided enough he could focus on his brother. Noah was looking at him with a smile on his face.

"Glad you could laugh at me," Noah pouted, then he burst into laughter.

Hunter and Noah laughed for quite a while before they settled down enough to realize they either had to eat lightly or take a chance the bears might come back if they tried to catch fish. After no sign of the bears for a few minutes, the boys decided the bears were more afraid of laughter in trees than the boys were of bears. Hunter climbed down with the solar oven and caught fish while Noah kept lookout from above. The rest of the night went without incident, and they went to bed with full tummies.

8

DAY FIVE ALONE

The sky was clear and warm when Hunter opened his eyes. He guessed they slept an hour or two longer than normal. *Yesterday's excitement took more out of us than we realized,* he thought. As Hunter stirred, Noah began to awaken also. The boys lay quietly, enjoying the sounds of the birds waking. Noah was the first to break the silence and asked if Hunter was hungry.

"Are you asking if I want to make you breakfast?" asked Hunter.

"Only if you want to," answered Noah.

Hunter didn't look at Noah. He closed his eyes and thought about how often Mom closes her eyes before answering Noah, and he now understood why.

"If you climb down and catch the fish, I will come down and cook them," said Hunter.

Noah was half down the tree before Hunter realized he'd

left. *I guess he's hungry,* thought Hunter as he got up to gather his gear.

After breakfast, the boys walked down to the dry riverbed and looked around. Hunter thought about walking down there, but the dry riverbed was more difficult to walk than the flat area along the irrigation culvert. He also didn't feel as safe far away from the culvert since their bear scare. After looking around and relaxing for four hours, the boys collected some food and returned to the tree. The boys had been stressed, walking quite a bit, and not sleeping well the last five days. They talked about it and decided to lie down in their nest for an afternoon nap.

Hunter was sleeping deeply when he was startled awake by a strange sound. It was far off, but he was sure he knew what it was. It sounded like a large group of Sasquatch walking below. Hunter crawled over to where Noah was and whispered for him to wake up. As Noah opened his eyes, he saw Hunter and quickly realized something was wrong. Hunter was holding his finger to his lips, letting him know to be quiet. As Noah woke up more, he heard the noise and remembered it well. Hard to forget the sound of a dozen eight-foot Sasquatch walking twenty feet below you.

The boys crawled to the edge of their nest and looked below. It looked like the same group of Sasquatch that had passed by yesterday were returning. The Sasquatch were still four hundred feet away, but they made enough noise they could hear them from where they were. While they were looking at the approaching Sasquatch, Noah suddenly turned around and began listening intently.

Hunter was trying to figure out what Noah was doing when

he heard it, too. After five days, they could hear Grandpa's crawler. The time in the woods alone taught them to be silent and listen before they moved or talked, but it didn't stop them from getting excited.

Hunter grabbed Noah's arm. "We can't make a sound," he whispered, "If we try to call Grandpa, we will all get caught."

The look in Noah's eyes told Hunter he understood but wasn't happy. Hunter knew he could trust his brother to be silent until the Sasquatch passed.

"After the Sasquatch have passed by safely, we will climb down and run to catch Grandpa." He instructed. Noah agreed. "I'm going over to watch the Sasquatch. Noah, you keep an eye on Grandpa," Hunter gestured toward where they could hear Grandpa.

Hunter lay back down to watch the Sasquatch approach. Fifty feet from the boy's tree, six of the twelve Sasquatch stopped while the others kept walking. Hunter watched with disbelief at six Sasquatch as they sat down and began eating the fruit they were carrying. Hunter crawled back to Noah and whispered into his ear what was happening. From the look on Noah's face, Hunter thought Noah was going to jump down to the Sasquatch again. Instead, Noah covered his mouth to stop himself from screaming.

Hunter headed back to watch the Sasquatch eat while Noah watched Grandpa slowly approach. Hunter watched Noah become more nervous and realized Grandpa must be going by. Hunter was sure Noah was becoming worried and moved over to his side. Sure enough, Grandpa had gone by already. Hunter realized he needed to keep Noah calm and reassured him they would be fine. He put his arm around Noah and held him tight as Grandpa disappeared.

After a minute, Noah quietly exclaimed, "I wished I could kick some Sasquatch for making us miss Grandpa."

With Grandpa out of sight, the two boys went to the other side of the nest to watch the Sasquatch. It was dark by the time the Sasquatch left, which was three hours after Grandpa had passed by. Hunter and Noah talked after the Sasquatch left. Both boys knew it would be unsafe to travel at night, even with the lights Grandpa built into their Carhartt coveralls. Instead, they ate a small dinner, climbed down to the culvert to wash up and returned to their nests to sleep. They decided they would eat a quick breakfast, then start running downstream to catch Grandpa first thing in the morning.

9

JUST MISSED

As he was unknowingly driving past his grandsons, Grandpa thought he was three or four days behind the boys and decided to move quickly to catch up. He hoped the boys would keep marking their sleeping trees so he could track them easily.

Only wish they had added dates, he thought as he drove the walker down the dry riverbed. He drove on until it was too dark to see, then stopped for the night. Grandpa did not know how close he was to the boys but would have been proud of how they acted under the difficult situation they went through, even if it meant they missed him.

10

DAY SIX

Grandpa woke up at first light and headed downstream, searching for the boys. He had been sleeping in the crawler since the boys had been taken. It allowed him to be safe and move out quickly if needed. Yesterday, not only had he missed seeing the boys, but he also missed the second tree the boys slept in and its message. He would have to add bright orange ribbon to the suits for the future. That is, if his son ever trusted him around the boys again.

Grandpa wouldn't have felt as guilty had he known about the dangers before leaving. He would never have allowed his grandsons to stay if he had known about the risks. He would have taken them home at once after they came out of hiding. His son's company will end up bearing the brunt of responsibility.

While Grandpa was driving further away, the boys were just waking. For safety, they needed to wait for full light before they could begin. The terrain was unpredictable, and sometimes predators were out, and the last thing they needed was to meet a bear or mountain lion in the dark. They ate, packed their gear, and relaxed while they waited. When it was light enough, they climbed down to wash.

Hunter decided they would start running and then take a break when needed. While they were resting, they could gather some food to munch on. They didn't want to waste time gathering since they wouldn't be resting in a tree all day. They were also going to stay on the hill by the irrigation culvert. They had a better view of the dry riverbed from above, and they felt it had a surface that was smoother to travel on. After the bear encounter, neither boy felt comfortable down in the open anymore.

Hunter figured they had jogged for ten miles without seeing or hearing any sign of Grandpa and slowed to a walk.

"I'm fine," said Noah, although he was breathing heavily.

Hunter knew Noah could normally run much further, but their Carhartt coveralls were a bit heavy and warm to run too far or fast in, so he called for a break.

They talked while Hunter made sure both drank enough water. They gathered a few berries as they rested, and after thirty minutes, Noah talked Hunter into starting again. Hunter agreed if Noah promised not to argue when he told him it was time to stop for the night. Noah agreed, and they started out again. This time, Noah said he would set the pace. Hunter let him, and they set off.

Hunter figured they had already jogged another eight miles at a faster pace than earlier. Noah's breathing was beginning to get faster and louder. He would let Noah run for another mile or two, then call it for the day. Noah started to argue, but as he slowed down to say something, he stumbled a bit. One look from Hunter was enough for Noah to keep silent and stop. He knew he was tired but didn't want to let Hunter down.

Once they stopped, Noah sat down, laid back, and sighed with relief, "Good call, brother."

Hunter figured they had run twenty miles that day. He knew Noah must be totally dead. Noah wasn't a competitive runner but was active and could normally run with Hunter for six to seven miles. Today showed Noah had more guts than Hunter would have believed. Hunter also knew his little brother was going to sleep soundly tonight. They both were going to sleep well. The stress of the situation was intense. Hunter was grateful he and Noah had all the survival training. As a young kid, it was playtime with Grandpa. Now that training is keeping them alive and ahead of the Sasquatch, he thought proudly.

The afternoon had been a bit cloudy, making running in coveralls easier, but the sky was too cloudy when it was time to cook dinner. The solar oven wouldn't work without enough sun, so the boys settled on their normal berries and mushrooms. While they were gathering berries, Noah spied a tree he thought might have nuts on it and called Hunter to come look. Hunter was very happy at Noah's find.

"Wow, Noah, do you know what that tree is?" asked Hunter.

"No idea," replied Noah.

"Well, Noah, that tree you found is a hazelnut tree, and yes, those are nuts on it!" said Hunter excitedly. "With luck, we will be able to fill a couple bags and eat like kings for days."

"I'm okay with any kind of nuts right now," said Noah. "I love fish, but I could use a day or two break before I eat another bite," he added.

The boys took long tree branches and hit the nut tree or pulled the branches down to pick the nuts. The boys filled three out of their four food bags. Noah decided they could gather the other stuff as they walked but might not find another nut tree, so they filled three bags, to his delight.

The boys ate nuts as they gathered. They peeled the outer skin off and cracked the shell. Most were ripe and Noah really did like the taste after days of fish. They filled the other bag with berries and dined on nuts and berries that night before crawling into their nests.

"This is scary," Noah whispered through the dark, "but in a way, it is a fun adventure. I know I will never forget this."

"I know what you mean, Noah," said Hunter, "It feels like a primitive test two cave boys would go through to become an adult."

"It is a good thing Dad and Grandpa were so into the woods, or we wouldn't be prepared," said Noah. "I might not want to do this again for a while, but I feel confident we will get home."

"Honestly, so do I," Hunter agreed, and he turned over to sleep for the night.

The boys built their nests lower in that night's tree in the event it rained. They wove small evergreen branches into the branches above each nest to give added protection from rain. There was just enough moonlight coming through the clouds to finish before they had to strap in for the night. Hunter could tell Noah fell asleep as soon as he laid down his weary head. He was also tired but knew his little brother must be much worse, but he was not saying a thing. *I will wait until tomorrow to see how we are feeling,* thought Hunter. *If we, or especially Noah, are too tired, we will rest for the day.* Hunter's last thought before he fell asleep was that Grandpa would come back for them, he relaxed and fell asleep.

11

DAY SEVEN

Grandpa awoke early and had been driving for three hours when he decided it was time for him to stop looking for the boys and go for help. He thought he at least could drive far enough to regain cell and radio reception. He was not having any luck without his electronic equipment. He knew the boys were also having the same issues, and he felt the time was now to head out. He hoped to find the boys when he came back but now needed to call for help. With thoughts of the boys on his mind, Grandpa headed away from the Sasquatch hidden valley.

When the boys woke up, the sun was out, and things were drying from the light rain during the night. Neither boy got so much as a drop on them. The tree branches were thick, and the extra cover they added was perfect for keeping the rain off.

Hunter saw how light it was around the tree and decided they were going to take a rest day. If they had not caught

Grandpa yesterday, then that meant he was driving fast. *Grandpa must have thought he was days behind us and had to go fast to catch us, or he was going for help. Either way, he will be back,* thought Hunter.

Hunter looked over at Noah and said, "I think we should find the perfect tree and stay in one place until Grandpa finds us. We have everything we need right here. We are safe, Grandpa knows we are close by, we can put obvious signs down on the dry riverbed that Grandpa and other rescuers won't miss."

Noah rolled onto his back, crossed his arms, thought for a moment, then said, "I'm okay with that." He rolled back over, "That means we need the perfect Sasquatch-proof tree," he added.

Hunter looked at Noah and laughed. He knew he had made the right decision to stay and was grateful that Noah felt comfortable with it.

"After we eat, it looks like we're going to have to spend some time finding that perfect tree, Noah," added Hunter.

"We need to find a tree that we can build escape routes out of," said Noah. "Maybe we could weave rope out of tree bark and make extra escape rope slides."

"I hope we aren't here long enough to need woven rope slides, but while we have time to kill waiting to be saved, then we might as well have fun and build a super fort," Hunter unclipped his safety lines and stood. "Times a wasting, little brother, let's climb down and start searching."

Noah watched his brother disappear and thought about how scared he was. It wasn't fair for him to make Hunter worry about him, so he would try his best to keep a calm face. The new fort was going to be amazing, but he would make sure no bears or Sasquatch would be able to get in. With that last thought, he unclipped and followed his brother below.

While the boys were looking for the perfect tree, Noah called to Hunter to come check something out. When Hunter got to him, Noah had a couple pieces of metal in his hand.

"Guess where I found these," Noah stated.

"Not a clue," replied Hunter.

"Inside a pocket in my arm sleeves," said Noah, "and I think they make something."

Hunter looked at the metal pieces, "Where did you find them?"

Noah pointed out a seam on each shoulder that had a Velcro tab sticking out, "The left one opened when I was sliding. A branch pushed it open and when I saw the metal, I pulled, and it came out. The other side had a tab also and another piece of metal. At first, I thought they were to protect us from getting hurt, but now I think they make something."

Hunter looked at the metal in Noah's hands for a moment, thinking. He then asked Noah to hand the parts to him, which Hunter studied for a minute before announcing he knew what they were. He looked at Noah and told him to take off his center harness cover.

Noah wasn't sure what Hunter was thinking as he handed his cover over.

Hunter looked at the parts, rotating them and tried to push them together a couple of times until Noah heard a click and

Hunter let out a "Yes!" Hunter then did a few more rotations, and Noah heard another click.

Hunter stood up, "I figured it out!"

He knew it was totally great.

Noah was looking at the now assembled thing in Hunter's hands, still unsure what it was, when Hunter pushed and held it up to Noah.

"What?" asked Noah.

"It's a slingshot!" Hunter cheered. "We must use one of your sleeping safety cords for the string to make it complete."

Noah grabbed the slingshot from Hunter's hand, detached a sleeping cord from his Carhartt coveralls, and giggled as he assembled it.

"This is the coolest ever," said Noah as he searched for a rock to try.

While Noah was trying out his new toy, he checked the shoulder seams of his Carhartt. Just as he thought Grandpa had included metal parts in his seams as well. While pulling out the parts, Hunter noticed the parts were bigger and there were more parts. After all the parts were out and lying on the ground, Hunter stared and thought. After two minutes, a smile slowly came to his lips.

"Dang, Grandpa is awesome," said Hunter as he began assembling the parts he had taken out of his coveralls. After he had all the parts together, Hunter stood back, looking with the biggest grin. He was going to have fun with this, he thought.

Noah was still shooting rocks while Hunter figured out where in his Carhartt's the rest of the parts were where he needed to make his new find work. Hunter found the needed string around his waist attached to his belt. He found the arrows in pouches on his legs. When completely assembled, Hunter had a crossbow with six arrows. Hunter figured Grandpa knew the boys would find the new items when needed, and for certain, they were needed now.

Noah's slingshot could shoot nuts and fruit out of trees or even launch a safety rope over a branch. Grandpa was not a hunter, so the slingshot was most likely a toy and a tool. The crossbow in Hunter's coveralls, though, was definitely a tool. Yes, it had applications like launching ropes as well, but Hunter was sure that Grandpa had intended it to be used for protection or hunting. The only arrow tips were sharp. There were no blunt arrow tips that could be used for work. Hunter felt proud that Grandpa had felt he was mature enough to be trusted with the crossbow. Hunter stored the arrows back into the leg seam pouches. The arms to the crossbow folded, and Hunter found clips on his shoulders for attaching the crossbow to his back while walking.

Noah stopped shooting rocks and looked at Hunter after all the arrows were stored and the crossbow strapped to his back. It took Noah almost two hours to notice the crossbow on Hunter's back and another three hours for Hunter to get him to stop asking to shoot it. Hunter explained they only had six arrows and they were all for hunting or protection, not playing. Noah wasn't happy, but after Hunter said they could shoot all the arrows when they were saved, he let it go and went back to shooting rocks with his slingshot. Hunter was wondering what was in the leg seams of Noah's Carhartt's, but by no means was going to search. He would wait and see if Noah found it himself.

12

DAY TEN

Grandpa had been driving 16 hours a day for three days, trying to find a way out of the valley. He was exhausted and without his electronics, he had no maps to guide him. Next time he would build a drone, he thought. As he came around a bend, he realized he had been there before. Which should have been impossible since he had been heading downstream for three days. He knew for sure it was the same spot because there was a tree across the dry riverbed with a deep gouge on it. Two days earlier, his walker's leg dragged hard across a log. Grandpa knew for sure it was the same log. He had gotten out to look at the walker's leg after hitting the log and saw the deep gouge. He sat looking at the log for over ten minutes, trying to figure out what had happened.

The walker has a manual altimeter gauge and manual attitude indicator. Grandpa was certain the attitude indicator always showed he was going downhill since leaving three days ago. There was no other choice but to start out again. This time, he kept eyes on not just the attitude indicator but note the altimeter reading as he went. After a deep sigh, Grandpa drove the crawler and climbed over the log again, leaving another deep gouge. As the log faded into the distance, Grandpa wondered what he should do if he saw this log one more time. Guess we'll cross that bridge if we get to it, thought Grandpa as he drove the crawler down the dry riverbed.

The boys found the perfect tree three days earlier. Or "trees" are more correct. The boys had found a group of six trees. Three trees on each side of the Sasquatch wall. The trees had branches that were interwoven, so all six connected. The boys spent the last three days weaving the branches together even closer so they could safely walk around. Noah had tried making rope from bark but decided it was too much work. Plus, there was doubt it could hold his weight.

They made two separate cooking platforms. One in the east for cooking in the morning sun and one in the west for the evening sun. There were over a dozen ways down the trees, each in a different direction. They even thought of ways to block bears from climbing up by adding woven branch gates that can open and be locked across the walkway branches. Half a dozen dedicated sleeping nests were scattered around the trees, giving different vantage points depending on the situation's needs. The boys had many other plans, depending on how long it took to be rescued.

The boys were setting up the food trees, which were separate from their nest tree. It was not wise to keep food in your car, tent, or tree with bears around. While they were attaching baskets, Noah suggested that they could stay there every summer after they were rescued.

Hunter looked at Noah and shook his head, "I might miss next year. I might need a vacation from this kind of vacation."

After Noah had fallen asleep, Hunter thought about their situation. He would give Grandpa and other rescuers one more week to find them. If no one showed up in a week, they would start moving again. They didn't have extra clothes, and the things they were wearing would not last much longer with the rough use they were getting. There was no way they would survive the winter either. Even if they found a cave that stored enough food, it got too cold up here in the mountains to survive without heat. If they started a fire, the Sasquatch would notice and capture them immediately. No, thought Hunter, in a week, they would leave. Until then, he and Noah would continue building and modifying their tree fort to keep busy.

13

17 DAYS

Grandpa slowed his speed in the crawler, limited daily driving time to less than eight hours a day, and only drove during the light. He didn't want to take the chance of missing his grandsons. The slower pace allowed him to look closer for the kids and try to decide what was happening with his instruments. He indeed reached the log with the two deep gouges again, much to his wonder. It took 4 days at the slower pace until he came upon it. That was three days ago, and most of the days since have been spent experimenting with heading in different directions. Grandpa had tried climbing up and down every place that looked promising, and it gave him chances to examine how the instruments acted. His best guess was he was in some sort of impossible loop.

His instruments showed he was going downhill, but he kept going in a giant circle. What became apparent on the first day of testing seven days ago was the instruments were not registering properly. They appeared to work, but the altimeter gauge never changed, no matter how high or low he drove. It always showed an altitude of 1232 feet. It was a manual gauge and used air pressure, so it should not be affected by anything. Obviously, the altimeter wasn't functioning properly, and the attitude gauge had stumped him as well.

Seven days ago, when Grandpa realized the altimeter gauge was broken, he found that the attitude gauge was also not working. It always showed the crawler going downhill, even if it was going uphill. He made a plumb bob out of a small rock and piece of string to test the gauge. He tied the string to the roof of the crawler so it hung down next to the attitude indicator. If the crawler went uphill, the rock should angle towards the back of the crawler and to the front if it was going downhill due to gravity. The angle of the string and rock plumb bob never changed.

Regardless of whether he was crawling up a steep hill or going down, the string always tilted slightly towards the front as though the crawler was going downhill. It went against physics for the string and rock not to follow gravity. If he had used metal instead of a rock, a magnetic field could affect the angle, but it was a rock. Grandpa even tried a few different rocks to be sure, with each acting the same.

Had it not been for the log with the gouge, Grandpa might have never noticed the instruments were acting up. If it hadn't been for the testing, Grandpa wouldn't have discovered something that defies the laws of gravity. This was the most amazing discovery imaginable, but would he ever find his grandsons and a way out of this mess to let someone know of his discovery? Having found an incredible scientific discovery is great, but it wouldn't mean a thing if he couldn't get out of this loop. Grandpa was thinking he might have to try going over the wall into the valley on foot if he couldn't figure out the crazy loop puzzle.

Hunter and Noah spent the last seven days building more details into their tree house. Noah insisted they make covered crows nests they could sleep in and shoot enemies without being seen. Hunter wasn't worried about enemies, but keeping Noah busy was important. They finally reached the seven-day limit Hunter set without being rescued. Now, it was time to let Noah know they were going to start following the culvert down-hill again.

Noah was leaning over the edge of a crow's nest right above the culvert, watching the water swirl, when Hunter approached and let him know it was time to leave.

"I was wondering when we were going," said Noah. "I love it here, but kind of miss Mom, Dad, and I bet Grandpa is very worried."

"You're right, Noah. I bet Grandpa is about to have a heart attack worrying," said Hunter. "We are doing fine, but Grandpa has no idea, so we need to get moving now. No one has shown up searching for us, so either Grandpa is still here trying to find us, or something has happened to him. Regardless, it is time we start heading out, and I miss Mom and Dad too," Hunter added. He didn't want Noah to feel bad for missing their parents, especially since he felt the same.

The boys gathered their things, ensured their tree was secured and headed out. Noah wanted to make sure their tree would make it through the winter so they could stay there again. They would continue to follow the irrigation culvert in hopes it would lead to a city or at least a farm. Noah and Hunter's main concerns were the Sasquatch and staying unseen while traveling. They would travel along the culvert but further down the hill by the dry riverbed. Hunter wanted to stay as far away from the Sasquatch as possible when they could. He also thought there would be less chance of missing him if they were down by the riverbed and Grandpa came by. The riverbed would be tougher to walk on but maybe safer.

Unknown to the boys, the decision to travel along the dry riverbed put them in the same crazy loop Grandpa was in. Had they stayed by the irrigation culvert, they would have been able to head down the valley toward a town like the water did. The Sasquatch did not want to draw unnecessary attention, so they let the water flow unaffected. By dropping into the dry riverbed, they were trapped.

At the exact moment the boys headed downstream in the dry riverbed, Grandpa had decided to turn around and head downstream. They were now all heading in the same direction, but possibly days apart.

Grandpa had spent days trying to get to the boys or out of the dry riverbed, it was time to try heading downstream again. He was running out of options and, for the life of him, could not figure out why his son's company had not sent out a search party for him. At this time, they should realize that not only was he missing, but his grandsons were also. It should be an easy jump to conclude they were with him. *Either way, where was the search party*, he wondered as he headed downstream. With all the weird things that had happened since they met the Sasquatch, Grandpa wondered if they had sent a search party and it had been captured by the Sasquatch. That was the only explanation that there hadn't been a rescue attempt.

14

NOAH GOES SWIMMING

It had been three days since the boys started walking. Three days without an incident until they came around a bend and saw two Sasquatch standing by a tree four hundred feet away. The boys saw the Sasquatch before the Sasquatch saw them and hid behind trees. The Sasquatch were looking downstream and missed the boys. Hunter signaled to Noah to crawl up towards the irrigation culvert. It took an hour to crawl the four hundred feet to the culvert. They kept watching the two Sasquatch by the riverbed as they crawled.

It took a few minutes to find a good spot to climb to the top of the culvert. They found a small drain ditch under the culvert and went in. Hunter went first, followed by Noah. Just as Noah could see the light coming under the other side of the culvert, Hunter had stopped. Noah kept pushing and complaining until Hunter moved and he could climb out from under the concrete culvert. Noah stood up and had started to ask Hunter what his problem was when he saw why Hunter had stopped. They had come out right in the middle of a group of Sasquatch.

The Sasquatch had the boys surrounded. There were over a dozen of the bug furry things around them. The boys had been backed up to the irrigation culvert. The Sasquatch knew the boys had not been in the water since the first time they had been captured, so they were completely taken by surprise at Noah's next move.

Noah looked at the Sasquatch around him, and stuck out his tongue, "Not this time, suckers!" and fell backward into the water laughing.

Hunter's eyes widened in surprise, but he quickly followed Noah into the water. By the time he was able to look back at the Sasquatch, Hunter saw that they still had not moved. *The Sasquatch are very afraid of water, so they froze,* thought Hunter as he caught up to Noah.

Noah was laughing when Hunter came up to his side. "Did you see their faces as I fell backward into the water?" Noah said while laughing.

Hunter looked at his brother and shook his head in disbelief. *How can this ten-year-old have so much confidence, or is he just crazy,* he thought.

The water where the boys went in was moving fast, and they had gone downhill for three miles before Noah said he was getting too cold to stay in the water. They had not been able to seal his waterproof boot seam, so Noah's pant leg was filling with freezing water. Hunter found a good tree to climb out of the water into so Noah could dry safely, and they headed up. Hunter knew the area they had traveled through was too rough for the sasquatch to follow. He did not expect them for hours, if not days. With luck, they may think the boys were still in the water and travel past looking for them.

The boys climbed high enough to be unseen from below and found an open sunny area where Noah could take off his Carhartt's so they could dry. While Noah sat in the sun to warm up, Hunter looked at him and pushed his shoulder playfully, "Nice job, little brother."

Noah gave his silly grin. "Did you see their eyes when I fell backward?"

"I sure did," said Hunter.

Luck was finally with the boys. They had chosen the same spot where Grandpa was. He was stopped and was scanning the area with his binoculars when he saw movement on the irrigation culvert. He about screamed out when he saw it was Noah and Hunter climbing out of the water up a tree.

Grandpa climbed the hill to the bottom of the tree the boys had climbed. He picked up two rocks and started hitting them together to get the boys' attention. Grandpa had taught the boys to use rocks or sticks to signal in the woods. If you called out, a predator would know you were human. Sticks and rocks could be anything.

The boys cautiously looked down and almost fell out of the tree when they saw Grandpa. Grandpa signaled for them to be silent and that he would climb to them. As he climbed, Grandpa was pleased with the tree the boys had picked. It was big enough to offer shelter and keep them safe, plus the water below was an added benefit. *Floating downstream was brilliant,* he thought, *but why were they still here after all this time? It must be the same forcefield.*

After many hugs and a few tears, Grandpa and the boys shared stories. They were about to help Noah out of his wet Carhartt's when the group of Sasquatch showed up below the tree and saw the three of them. Grandpa told the boys to keep still.

The Sasquatch were gathering by the tree base when Noah told Grandpa that the Sasquatch couldn't swim and they should all jump back in and float into the next state.

"The only problem we have," said Hunter, "is Noah has a hole in his boot seam and gets too cold to float for too long."

Grandpa looked at Hunter and asked if it was true that the Sasquatch couldn't swim.

"Noah and I have jumped in a few times, and they have never followed us," said Hunter.

Grandpa looked at the Sasquatch below, then at his grandsons, and said, "Oh, what the heck, the culvert must be better than sitting in a tree with a dozen Sasquatch waiting below."

The three looked at one another, smiled, and then, as one, jumped into the culvert. Grandpa and Hunter held Noah's leg up out of the water to keep it drier. It was the last they saw of the Sasquatch. After what Grandpa guessed was two hours, his watch began to vibrate, letting him know they were now getting an occasional signal. Noah wasn't cold, so they continued to float until they went under a bridge.

They had been floating on their backs, and Hunter sat up to look. They floated into a small town in Eastern Washington.

Grandpa and the boys climbed out of the culvert and headed to the gas station to get help and call the boys' dad.

"What's wrong, boys? Where are you? How did you get with Grandpa?" Dad asked, fretting with worry.

The boys try to explain, "We snuck aboard Grandpa's crawler seventeen days ago after hearing about his trip."

"That is ridiculous, Grandpa has only been out of radio contact for ten minutes."

Grandpa explained that the town they were calling from was fifty miles from where they went ten minutes ago, so that would have been impossible. After five minutes of questions, the company lab director told the three to wait, and he would send a helicopter to pick them up. Three hours later, the company had picked them up and taken them to the lab for questioning.

While Grandpa and the two boys were being questioned, a lab tech viewing the security films of Grandpa in the lab that morning noticed Grandpa was clean-shaven, and yet he had over two weeks of growth a few hours later. The tech called the lab director to check out the tape. The director looked at the film and asked to see all the electronic equipment Grandpa and the boys had during the period they were gone.

After analyzing the phones, smartwatches, and smart glasses of the two boys and Grandpa, the lab was able to determine the three had been somewhere for seventeen days when only ten minutes had passed in the real world. There were incidences when their electronic equipment received enough random signals to record a date and time.

A final examination of the evidence confirmed what

happened in the valley over the seventeen days shown on the electronics and personal reports. The experts determined the only explanation possible was that the Sasquatch had held them in a time bubble. The only possible way to know for sure was for a large, well-equipped research team to head back to the valley. Goings determined that going into the Sasquatch Valley up the irrigation culvert would be the safest and easiest access.

"Looks like we must go back," said Noah, he clicked his toe blades out, the same ones he had used trying to kick the Sasquatch, and added, "I am ready to kick Sasquatch butt again."

The room erupted with laughter, Noah's dad looked at Grandpa and said, "I could see Noah doing that."

Grandpa smiled, knowing Noah was exactly like his father.

ABOUT THE AUTHOR

Patrick Talmadge Sr. has always been a late bloomer. His growth didn't cease until he was over 21 years old. He reached his pinnacle as a national and world-class masters middle-distance runner at the age of 37, when he won his first master's national track and field championship in the 800-meter run.

At 47, Patrick earned his Bachelor of Arts degree and made history as the oldest NCAA cross-country runner. Seven years later, at 54, he returned to college to pursue a Master's degree in Psychology. During this time, he ran the mile in track, once again setting a record as the oldest NCAA track and field runner. He received his Master's degree in Psychology at 57. At the age of 66, he embarked on his writing journey.

Patrick taught himself to read at the tender age of three and a half and has been an avid reader ever since. With a keen interest in all fields of science, science fiction, and fantasy, he amassed a wealth of knowledge that would later prove invaluable when he began writing. Throughout his 20s and 30s, Patrick devoured two to three books a day. Upon graduating from graduate school in 2011, he retired from competitive running and felt a growing desire to write the stories that had been simmering within him.

In November 2021, spurred on by the love of his life, Patrick began his writing career. By July 2023, he had completed an adult four-book science fiction series about Sasquatch, a four-book children's series on the same subject, and a standalone novel about a senior community that befriends a troupe of Sasquatch.

Patrick possesses a unique ability to write multiple stories simultaneously, allowing him to modify and adjust interconnected narratives for clarity when writing a series. With a bit of luck, Patrick will continue to pursue his passion for writing for the rest of his life, or at least until his computer gives out.

ALSO BY PATRICK TALMADGE

Hidden Mountain Chronicles

Sasquatch Race

Sasquatch Prison Diary

Tenino Caverns

Sasquatch Home Planet

Sasquatch Chronicles

Hunter and Noah vs. Sasquatch Vol. 1

Hunter and Noah vs. Sasquatch Vol. 2

Hunter and Noah vs. Sasquatch Vol. 3

Hunter and Noah vs. Sasquatch Vol. 4

Sasquatch Senior Community Series

Sasquatch Senior Community

Sasquatch Senior Community: Lois and Mel the Beginning

Sasquatch Senior Community: The Early Years

Sasquatch Senior Community: The Middle Years

AFTERWORD

Go to hangar1publishing.com to learn more about the Authors and stay up to date with their newest releases.